To Jerri, my biggest cheerleader—A.G.

For my mushroom-loving Dad—V.S.

Text copyright © 2024 by Alisha Gabriel
Illustrations copyright © 2024 by Vivien Sárkány

First Edition

This is a work of fiction. Names, characters, places and incidents are either the product of the author's imagination or are used fictitiously. Any resemblance to current events, locales, or living persons is entirely coincidental. No part of this book may be reproduced, transmitted in any form or by any means, electronic, mechanical, photocopying, recording, or otherwise, or stored in a retrieval system without permission in writing from the author. The publisher does not have any control over and does not assume any responsibility for author or third party websites or their content.

No part of this book may be used or reproduced in any manner for the purpose of training artificial intelligence technologies or systems, including but not limited to machine learning models, generative artificial intelligence, large language models (LLMs), etc.

The artwork was created digitally.

ISBN: 978-1-998426-08-9 (hbk.)
ISBN: 978-1-998426-09-6 (pbk.)
ISBN: 978-1-998426-07-2 (ebk.)

Tielmour Press books are available at special quantity discount to retailers, professional associations, schools and literacy programs, and other organizations. For details and discount information, contact us at: sales@tielmourpress.com

No generative AI was used in the production of this book.

Library and Archives Canada Cataloguing in Publication

Title: Fungi are... : more than mushrooms / words by Alisha Gabriel ; art by Vivien Sárkány.
Names: Gabriel, Alisha, author | Sárkány, Vivien, illustrator.
Identifiers: Canadiana (print) 20240489454 | Canadiana (ebook) 20240489462 | ISBN 9781998426089 (hardcover) | ISBN 9781998426096 (softcover) | ISBN 9781998426072 (EPUB)
Subjects: LCSH: Fungi—Ecology—Juvenile literature. | LCSH: Fungi—Juvenile literature. | LCGFT: Informational works. | LCGFT: Instructional and educational works. | LCGFT: Picture books.
Classification: LCC QK604.2.E26 G33 2025 | DDC j579.5—dc23

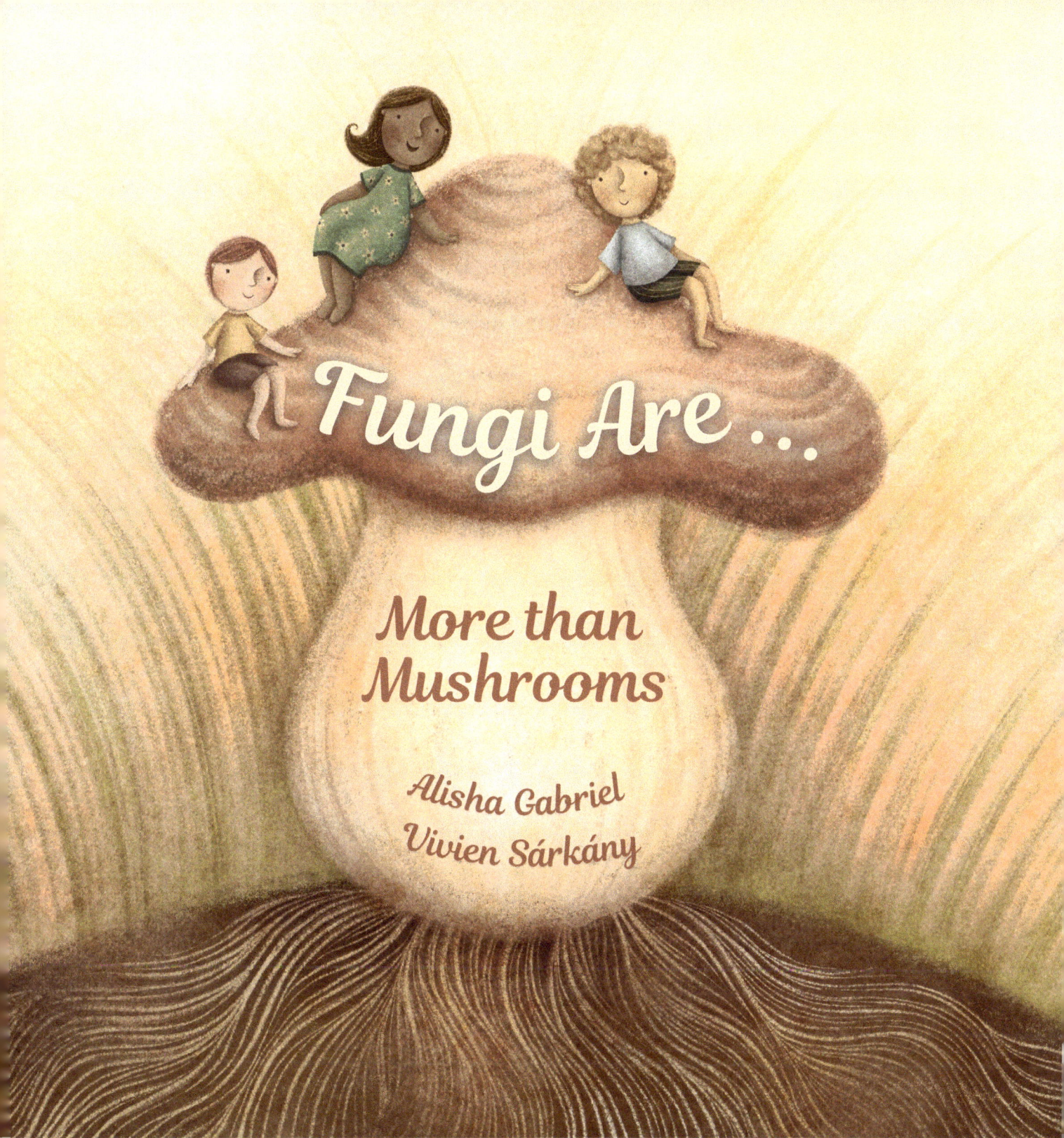

Fungi are travelers.

When rain plops on a puffball mushroom, its spores rise and float from its center like smoke from a chimney.

They burst,

Texas star mushrooms look like small cigars until they burst open with a hiss, splitting into a star shape to spread their spores.

fling,

The hat-thrower fungus shoots its spores fast and far like an arrow shot from a bow.

and grab.

Some spores stick to an animal's fur, or even our clothes, and end up in a new neighborhood or place.

Fungi are recyclers.

When it comes to fungi, dead plants and animals are on the menu. And it's a good thing, or our world would be piled high with leaves, branches, and animal remains.

They explore,

Spores land on the ground and send thinner-than-hair hyphae through the soil toward food.

break down,

The hyphae produce digestive enzymes to help decompose organic matter. They return nutrients they don't need to the soil for plants and other organisms to use.

and share.

About 90 percent of trees and plants form symbiotic relationships with fungi that live near their roots. The plants serve carbohydrates to their fungal guests, who pass back water and nutrients in return.

Fungi are homes.

Flies and gnats lay their eggs in mushrooms so their larvae are protected and surrounded by a handy food source.

They soften,

Red heart fungus weakens pine tree wood, making it easier for red-cockaded woodpeckers to drill holes for their nests.

cradle,

Ruby-throated hummingbirds cover and camouflage their nests with lichens.

and protect.

Shelf fungi keep rain out of this middle spotted woodpecker's nest.

Fungi are food.

Snails munch on mushrooms, deer and caribou nibble on lichens, and red squirrels store dry mushrooms in trees to eat during the winter!

They fluff,

Single-celled fungi known as yeasts digest the sugars in dough to make bread. This process produces little bubbles of carbon dioxide, which make the dough rise and become lighter and fluffier.

ferment,

Several types of fungi produce enzymes that ferment foods, which preserves the food and enhances its flavor and nutrition. Without fungi, we wouldn't have chocolate, blue cheese, soy sauce, miso, and more.

and nourish.

Mushrooms are not only yummy but also a nutritious source of protein and amino acids. They're also full of vitamin D, potassium, magnesium, calcium, and zinc.

Fungi hold the world together.

Mycelium is a mostly unseen underground network of fungal webs called hyphal threads. They bind the soil together to prevent erosion.

They clean,

Oyster mushrooms help clean up oil spills, some molds pull copper from the ground, and several types of fungi produce enzymes that digest plastic.

strengthen,

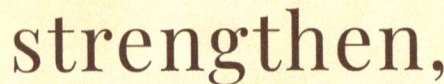

Extracts from amadou and reishi mushrooms can help honeybees fight off viruses to stay healthy.

and heal.

People have been foraging for fungi for better health for thousands of years. Penicillin is the best-known medicine derived from fungi—but it's not the only one. Even now, scientists are looking for new ways fungi can help cure diseases.

Fungi are unique.

From baskets to birds' nests and umbrellas to coral, the sizes, shapes, and colors of fungi are fantastical.

They are colorful,

The oxygen in the air turns some bolete mushrooms rainbow colors when they're scratched or cut.

aromatic,

Fungi can smell like rotting flesh, but also maple syrup, strawberries, and even watermelon!

and bioluminescent.

Over one hundred species of mushrooms become nature's nightlight when they glow in the dark.

Fungi are for wondering.

When you see a fuzzy patch of mold, a clump of lichen, or a mushroom in your garden, take a closer look. Most go unnoticed, quietly connecting the world, but fungi are...

more than mushrooms.

Did you see these items?

Try and find these items that were scattered throughout the story! Can you find all of them?

 Doll

 Owl

 Vase

 Butterfly

 Ladybug

 Hat

 Pencil

 Acorn

 Firefly

 Umbrella

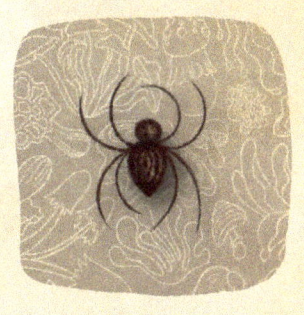 Spider

 Necklace

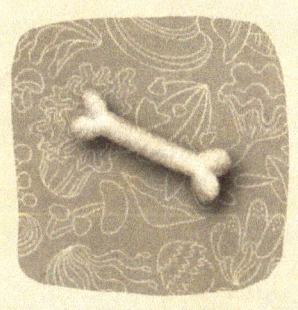 Bone

www.ingramcontent.com/pod-product-compliance
Lightning Source LLC
LaVergne TN
LVHW070220080526
838202LV00067B/6874